CRANBERRY THANKSGIVING

Wende and Harry Devlin

Aladdin Paperbacks

Aladdin Paperbacks
An imprint of Simon & Schuster
Children's Publishing Division
1230 Avenue of the Americas
New York, NY 10020
First Aladdin Paperbacks edition, 1990
Also available in a hardcover edition from
Simon & Schuster Books for Young Readers
Printed in Mexico
10

Library of Congress Cataloging-in-Publication Data
Devlin, Wende.
Cranberry Thanksgiving/Wende and Harry Devlin.
p.   cm.
Reprint. Originally published: New York: Parent's Magazine Press, 1971;
reissued Four Winds Press, 1980.
Grandmother almost loses her secret recipe for cranberry bread to one
of the guests she and Maggie invite for Thanksgiving dinner. Includes
the secret recipe.
ISBN 0–689–71429–7
[1. Bread—Fiction. 2. Thanksgiving Day—Fiction.] I. Devlin, Harry.
II. Title.
PZ7.D49875Ct   1990
[E]—dc20   89–18642   CIP   AC

To Todd Noel Devlin

Maggie darted about like a black-stockinged bird, in search of wood for the fireplace. She and her grandmother lived at the edge of a lonely cranberry bog in New England, and the winds were cold at the edge of the sea.

Today, Mr. Whiskers was helping Maggie with her chores and they soon had armfuls of firewood.

"Happy Thanksgiving Day, Mr. Whiskers." Maggie smiled at her friend.

That wasn't his real name of course. It was Uriah Peabody, but Maggie had called him Mr. Whiskers ever since she could remember. Maggie was very fond of Mr. Whiskers.

Her grandmother was not. "Too many whiskers and not enough soap," she often said to Maggie.

"Mr. Whiskers, indeed!" sniffed Grandmother, peeking from her kitchen window. She pulled the curtains tight again.

Whenever Grandmother baked her cranberry bread, she pulled her curtains tight. The reason for this was that her cranberry bread was the most famous for miles around.

It was so famous that bakers all over the countryside had offered great sums of money for the recipe. Although Grandmother scoffed at the whole idea, still she felt it was something wonderful to leave to Maggie.

She carefully hid the recipe behind a brick in the fire-place. "Oh, a lot of people would like to get that recipe," she fumed to herself, "especially Maggie's clam-digging friend, Mr. Whiskers."

Strange how he always showed up when she took down the great yellow bowl and all the good things that went into it.

"Scat! Shoo!" she would call out the window everytime he came too close to the house.

But forget all that today. It was Thanksgiving, her favorite day of the year. The cranberries had been picked, boxed and sent to the market. The dried corn had been soaked and the corn pudding made. The turkey was roasting in the old iron oven. Turnips, tiny green peas and a pumpkin pie were ready. The cranberry bread was cooling on the wooden board. The real work was done and the feast was almost ready.

Every year Grandmother invited a guest for dinner and allowed Maggie to do the same.

"Ask someone poor or lonely," she always said.

It never mattered to Maggie or her grandmother that the red carpet was worn and mended or that the silver spoons didn't match. Friendship and sharing were important. But everyone knew that.

Red-cheeked, Maggie raced into the house. While she changed, Grandmother excitedly told her whom she had invited. Mr. Horace was his name and he was staying at the Town Hotel.

"He actually bows, and he has a gold cane and smells of lavender," said Grandmother happily. "And he's all alone."

Maggie looked a little uncertain. "My guest doesn't smell of lavender," she began, "and he hasn't had a Thanksgiving dinner in twenty years. I invited Mr. Whiskers."

"Mr. Whiskers!" Grandmother didn't appear to believe she had heard right. "You mean here—in the house?"

But now there was a sound at the door and a loud clanging of the knocker.

"Quick, Grandmother—take off your apron."

Grandmother opened the door and there they were—both guests—Mr. Horace, pink-cheeked and starched, and Mr. Whiskers in his old captain's hat.

As they came in, trailing behind was the smell of lavender in an aura of clams and seaweed.

Mr. Whiskers held up his hands to Grandmother. "Clean," he said.

"Oh? And where is your tie?" Grandmother asked.

He lifted his long whiskers. "Right here where it's always been," he growled.

Maggie thought she saw a smile behind the whiskers. "Humph," said Grandmother, and taking Mr. Horace's arm, she led them into the dining room.

A log fire sputtered, the glasses shone, and certainly no one would notice that the silver spoons didn't match.

"Let's sing *We Gather Together*," said Maggie, trying to warm things up.

They all joined in the old hymn and midway began to sing out with cheer and gusto. Grandmother started to trill like a bird, until Mr. Whiskers fixed her with a quizzical gaze and shook his ears.

"How about *Sixteen Men on a Dead Man's Chest?*"
he roared, slapping his knee.

Mr. Horace looked pained.

Grandmother peered over her glasses. "Really," she said.

Maggie left the table and reappeared with the roast
turkey. The corn pudding, peas, cranberry jelly and turnips soon followed. And then came pale sweet butter and
Grandmother's famous cranberry bread.

"Feast of feasts," murmured Mr. Whiskers.

"Well, we have all heard about your cranberry bread," chuckled Mr. Horace, "and the recipe hidden in the kitchen fireplace."

"It's in the *dining-room* fireplace," said Grandmother, and looking over at Mr. Whiskers, she added, "and you, sir, will never find it!"

Mr. Whiskers stared at the turkey and pretended not to have heard her.

Maggie began to get nervous, but she made sure everyone was served some of each dish, and they began to eat.

What a great full dinner that was—with everything cooked with crisp edges and tender centers.

"How delicious!" said Maggie.

"How exquisite!" said Mr. Horace.

"How about some more?" said Mr. Whiskers.

At last they finished dinner, and Maggie and Grandmother cleared the table and went into the kitchen.

"Watch that Whiskers fellow," Grandmother whispered to Maggie.

Maggie opened the kitchen door just a small bit and peeked into the dining room. Her eyes widened.

"Grandmother! He's found it!"

Crash—clumpity!

There was a sound of wild scuffling, loud shouts and falling chairs.

Two figures pushed to the front door. For a moment they wrestled at the doorway and then seemed to burst into the purple dusk. One chased the other into the cranberry bog.

"The nerve of him, stealing our recipe," said Grandmother with fire in her eye.

Maggie knew whom she meant. "It wasn't Mr. Whiskers," she said, "it was Mr. Horace!"

"Mr. Horace!" Grandmother looked shocked. "But why?"

"Because he owns a bakery in the city."

"And Mr. Whiskers knew this?" Grandmother asked.

"Yes," said Maggie. "Mr. Whiskers kindly came today to watch Mr. Horace...and to have dinner."

Mr. Whiskers came puffing up to the door, holding Mr. Horace by the collar. Proudly he held the recipe high in the other hand.

"Don't trust a man because he smells of lavender and has a gold cane," he growled.

Grandmother stood up very straight and looked hard at
Mr. Horace. "You, sir," she said, "are a disgrace."
"He's worse that that," said Mr. Whiskers.
"He's a recipe robber," said Maggie.
All the starch seemed to leave Mr. Horace.

"No pumpkin pie for you, sir," said Grandmother, handing him his cane.

Mr. Horace began to sniffle.

They left Mr. Horace on the doorstep. Grandmother closed the door firmly and this time she took Mr. Whiskers' arm into the dining room. Maggie thought she could see Mr. Whiskers smile.

They sat by the warm embers of the fire and ate pumpkin pie with whipped cream.

"How delicious," said Maggie.

"How delightful," said Grandmother.
"How about another piece?" said Mr. Whiskers.
The wind blew and rattled the shutters, and outside the
door came a loud wail from Mr. Horace.

"Goodness! Is he still there?" said Maggie.

"Shall we let him in? It is Thanksgiving!" said Grand-mother.

"It's especially Thanksgiving on a cranberry farm," Maggie replied encouragingly.

They looked at Mr. Whiskers.

It took great effort on Mr. Whiskers' part. But with true character, he stood up and said, "Maggie, open the door and we shall give him the last piece."

"How about *Sixteen Men on a Dead Man's Chest?*" Grandmother asked him, while Maggie went to the door.
And even his whiskers couldn't hide *that* smile.

Grandmother's Famous Cranberry Bread

(Get Mother to help)

2 cups sifted all-purpose flour

1 cup sugar

1 ½ teaspoons baking powder

1 teaspoon salt

½ teaspoon baking soda

¼ cup butter or margarine

1 egg, beaten

1 teaspoon grated orange peel

¾ cup orange juice

1 ½ cups light raisins

1 ½ cups fresh or frozen cranberries, chopped

Sift flour, sugar, baking powder, salt, and baking soda into a large bowl. Cut in butter until mixture is crumbly. Add egg, orange peel, and orange juice all at once; stir just until mixture is evenly moist. Fold in raisins and cranberries.

Spoon into a greased 9 x 5 x 3-inch loaf pan. Bake at 350° for 1 hour and 10 minutes, or until a toothpick inserted in center comes out clean. Remove from pan; cool on a wire rack.

If you choose, you may substitute cranberries for the raisins to have an all cranberrry bread.

Recipe tested by the Food Department of Parents' Magazine